Learn

Practical Guide

A. De Quattro

Practical Guide

1.Introduction to Perl

Perl, which stands for "Practical Extraction and Reporting Language," is a high-level programming language created by Larry Wall in 1987. It is an extremely flexible and powerful language that has been used for various applications, including web development, scripting, system automation, data analysis, and much more. Perl is appreciated for its ease in text processing and its ability to efficiently handle multiple tasks.

Reasons to Learn Perl

There are many reasons to learn Perl. One of the main reasons is its versatility. Perl can be used to develop a wide range of applications, from simple to complex. It is widely used for text processing and automating repetitive tasks, but can also be used to create advanced web applications, analyze data, and much more. Learning Perl will give you the opportunity to tackle different projects and acquire new skills.

Another reason to learn Perl is its popularity and widespread use. Perl is one of the most widely used scripting languages in the world and is supported by a large community of developers who provide resources, documentation, and support. Knowing Perl will allow you to collaborate with other programmers and access a vast library of ready-to-use scripts.

Lastly, Perl is a very powerful programming language. With its flexible syntax and rich library of functions, Perl allows you to write efficient and clean code to solve complex problems. Learning Perl will help you become a more competent programmer and successfully manage projects of varying complexity.

Key Features of Perl

The main features of Perl are its ability to easily handle text processing, its flexibility, and its power. Thanks to its powerful string manipulation functions and support for regular expressions, Perl is ideal for processing text quickly and efficiently. It can be used to analyze text files, extract data from structured documents, create custom reports, and much more.

Perl is also known for its flexibility. It is an extremely dynamic language that allows programmers to write code easily and quickly. Its syntax is very intuitive and allows for expressing complex concepts clearly and concisely. Additionally, Perl supports multiple programming paradigms, including procedural programming, object-oriented programming, and functional programming.

Finally, Perl is a very powerful language. With its extensive library of built-in functions and its ability to integrate with other languages and systems, Perl can handle projects of varying sizes and complexity. It is used in many industries and sectors, including web development, bioinformatics, system automation, and much more.

Perl is an extremely versatile programming language that offers numerous possibilities to developers. Learning Perl will help you develop new skills, work on interesting projects, and collaborate with other programmers. If you are interested in improving your programming skills and exploring new professional opportunities, Perl could be the right language for you.

2. Perl Installation Guide

Before proceeding with the installation of Perl, it is important to familiarize yourself with the system requirements and prepare the environment for installation. In this chapter, detailed instructions will be provided on how to check the system requirements and prepare the system for Perl installation.

1.1 Checking System Requirements

Before starting the installation of Perl, make sure to check that your system meets the minimum requirements. The following are the recommended system requirements for installing Perl:

- Operating System: Perl is compatible with a wide range of operating systems, including Linux, macOS, and Windows. Make sure to use a supported operating system to ensure a proper installation of Perl.

- Disk Space: make sure you have enough disk space available for the installation of Perl and its additional modules. It is recommended to have at least 100 MB of disk space available for Perl installation.

- Memory: ensure you have an adequate amount of RAM to properly run Perl and the applications that rely on it. It is recommended to have at least 512 MB of RAM for an optimal experience.

- Other Requirements: make sure you have the necessary software and system packages required for Perl installation, such as a C compiler and the development libraries needed for compiling Perl modules.

Once the system requirements have been verified, you can proceed with preparing the system for Perl installation.

1.2 System Preparation

Before proceeding with the installation of Perl, it is advisable to perform some preparation operations to ensure a proper installation and configuration. The following are some recommended preparation operations:

- System Update: before installing Perl, make sure to update the operating system and all system packages to the latest version. This will help avoid errors during installation and ensure compatibility with the latest versions of Perl.

- Installation of Prerequisites: make sure to install all the prerequisites necessary for Perl installation, such as the C compiler and development libraries. These prerequisites are essential for compiling Perl modules and ensuring a smooth installation.

- Creation of a Dedicated User: it is advisable to create a dedicated user for Perl usage to limit security risks and ensure proper management of Perl scripts and applications. Make sure to assign the correct permissions to the dedicated user to access the necessary system resources.

- Firewall Configuration: if you are using a firewall on your system, make sure to configure it properly to allow access to Perl and the applications using it. Configure the firewall rules to allow incoming and outgoing traffic from the ports used by Perl.

With the system preparation completed, you are now ready to proceed with the installation of Perl. The next chapter will provide detailed instructions on how to download and install Perl on your operating system.

3. Basic Perl Syntax

The basic syntax of Perl is fundamental for writing scripts and programs in this versatile and powerful scripting language. Perl is an interpreted language, developed by Larry Wall in the 1980s, and has become one of the most popular languages for scripting, text processing, and web programming.

The basic syntax of Perl is based on fundamental principles such as variable declaration, the use of operators, function definition, and the use of control structures. Let's look at some details of the basic Perl syntax:

1. Variable declaration: in Perl, variables are declared simply by assigning them a value. For example, to declare a numerical variable the '$' symbol is used:

```perl
$number = 10;
```

To declare a string variable the '@' symbol is used:

```perl
$string = "Hello, world!";
```

It's important to note that Perl is a weakly typed language, which means it's not necessary to explicitly declare the type of a variable.

2. Operators: Perl supports a wide range of operators for performing mathematical, logical, and comparison operations. For example:

- Mathematical operators: +, -, *, /

- Logical operators: && (AND), || (OR), ! (NOT)

- Comparison operators: == (equal), != (not equal), > (greater than), < (less than)

Example of using operators in Perl:

```perl
$a = 10;
$b = 5;
$c = $a + $b; # addition
$d = $a > $b; # comparison
```

3. Function definition: functions in Perl are defined using the 'sub' keyword. For example, a simple function to get the sum of two

numbers could be defined as follows:

```perl
sub sum {
    my ($num1, $num2) = @_;
    return $num1 + $num2;
}
```

This function can then be called within the main code with the desired parameters:

```perl
$result = sum(10, 5); # $result will be equal to 15
```

4. Control structures: Perl supports classic control structures like 'if', 'else', 'elsif', and 'while' to manage the flow of program

execution. For example:

- If-else:

```perl
if ($value > 0) {
    print "The value is greater than zero
";
} else {
    print "The value is less than or equal to zero
";
}
```

- While:

```perl
```

```perl
$counter = 0;

while ($counter < 10) {

    print "The counter is $counter
";

    $counter++;

}
```

5. Comments: comments in Perl are inserted using the '#' symbol. All lines following the '#' symbol will be considered as comments and will not be executed by the compiler. For example:

```perl
# This is a comment in Perl

print "This is an example of a comment"; # This line of code will be executed
```

Additionally, Perl also supports multi-line comments using the '=pod' and '=cut' syntax:

```perl
=pod
This is a multi-line comment in Perl
=cut
```

The basic syntax of Perl is relatively easy to learn and understand, while offering great flexibility and power for writing scripts and programs. With its versatile nature and wide range of available libraries, Perl is a widely used language for scripting and automating processes. With a good command of the basic syntax of Perl, it is possible to create efficient and complex programs for a variety of applications.

4. Variables and Data Types in Perl

In Perl, variables are used to store and manipulate data within a program. Variables in Perl are defined using the symbol '$' followed by the variable name. For example, the following line of code defines a variable named $number that contains the value 10:

```
$number = 10;
```

Perl supports different data types, including:

1. Scalars: scalar variables can hold a single value, such as a number or a string. For example:

```
$name = "Alice";
$age = 25;
```

2. Array: array variables can hold an ordered list of values. Elements in an array in Perl are indexed starting from 0. For example:

```perl
@numbers = (1, 2, 3, 4, 5);
print $numbers[2]; # prints the third element of the array (3)
```

3. Hash: hash variables can hold a collection of key-value pairs. For example:

```perl
%student = ('name' => 'Bob', 'age' => 30);
print $student{'name'}; # prints the value associated with the key 'name' (Bob)
```

4. Variables again and refer: variables can also be redeclared using the 'my' symbol. For example:

```perl
my $greeting = "Hello";
```

my $greeting;

In Perl, data types are "weak", which means that it is not necessary to explicitly declare the type of a variable. However, variables can be typed using the following prefixes:

- $ for scalar variables

- @ for array variables

- % for hash variables

Here are some examples of variables and data types in Perl:

Scalar variable

$name = "Alice";

$age = 25;

Array variable

```perl
@numbers = (1, 2, 3, 4, 5);


# Hash variable

%student = ('name' => 'Bob', 'age' => 30);


# Using the variables

print "The student's name is $student{'name'}\n";

print "The second digit in the array is $numbers[1]\n";
```

It is important to note that in Perl, it is possible to convert one data type to another using conversion functions like int(), str(), etc. For example:

```perl
$number = "10";

$integer_number = int($number); # converts the string into an integer
```

Furthermore, Perl also offers some special data types like references. A reference is a data type that refers to another variable rather than directly containing the data. For example:

```
$number = 10;

$number_reference = \$number; #
$number_reference contains a reference to the
variable $number
```

With references, it is possible to efficiently pass variables to functions and create complex data structures like nested lists and trees.

Perl offers a wide range of data types and flexibility in using variables. With a good understanding of how to declare, initialize, and use variables in Perl, it is possible to create powerful and dynamic programs that easily handle a variety of data and operations.

5.Operators in Perl

In Perl, operators are special symbols or reserved words that are used to perform mathematical, logical, comparison, and other operations. Operators in Perl can be divided into various categories, including arithmetic operators, comparison operators, logical operators, assignment operators, and concatenation operators. In this guide, we will examine some of the most common operators in Perl, along with examples of how they can be used.

Arithmetic operators:

Arithmetic operators are used to perform mathematical operations on numbers. Some of the most common arithmetic operators in Perl include:

- + (addition): performs addition between two numbers.

Example:

```perl
my $sum = 5 + 3; # $sum will contain the
value 8
```

- - (subtraction): performs subtraction between two numbers.

Example:

```perl
my $diff = 10 - 5; # $diff will contain the
value 5
```

- * (multiplication): performs multiplication between two numbers.

Example:

```perl
my $prod = 6 * 4; # $prod will contain the
value 24
```

- / (division): performs division between two numbers.

Example:

my $quotient = 12 / 3; # $quotient will contain the value 4

- % (modulo): calculates the remainder of a division between two numbers.

Example:

my $remainder = 10 % 3; # $remainder will contain the value 1

Comparison operators:

Comparison operators are used to compare two values and determine if they are equal or not equal. Some of the most common comparison operators in Perl include:

- == (equal): determines if two values are equal.

Example:

my $x = 5;

my $y = 10;

```perl
if ($x == $y) {

    print "The two values are equal

";

} else {

    print "The two values are different

";

}
```

- != (not equal): determines if two values are not equal.

Example:

```perl
my $a = 2;

my $b = 2;

if ($a != $b) {

    print "The two values are different

";

} else {
```

```perl
    print "The two values are equal
";

}
```

- > (greater): determines if the first value is greater than the second.

Example:

```perl
my $num1 = 8;

my $num2 = 4;

if ($num1 > $num2) {

    print "The first number is greater than the second
";

} else {

    print "The first number is not greater than the second
";

}
```

- < (less): determines if the first value is less than the second.

Example:

```
my $val1 = 10;

my $val2 = 15;

if ($val1 < $val2) {

    print "The first value is less than the second
";

} else {

    print "The first value is not less than the second
";

}
```

Logical operators:

Logical operators are used to combine or invert logical values. Some of the most common logical operators in Perl include:

- && (logical and): returns true if both values are true.

Example:

```perl
my $a = 1;

my $b = 0;

if ($a && $b) {

    print "Both values are true
";

} else {

    print "At least one of the values is false
";

}
```

- || (logical or): returns true if at least one of the values is true.

Example:

```
my $x = 10;

my $y = 0;

if ($x || $y) {

    print "At least one of the values is true
";

} else {

    print "Both values are false
";

}
```

- ! (not): inverts the logical value of a variable.

Example:

```
my $flag = 0;

if (!$flag) {
```

```
    print "The flag is false
";
} else {
    print "The flag is true
";
}
```

Assignment operators:

Assignment operators are used to assign values to variables. Some of the most common assignment operators in Perl include:

- = (assignment): assigns a value to a variable.

Example:

my $num = 10; # $num will contain the value 10

- += (addition-assignment): adds a value to an existing variable.

Example:

my $count = 5;

$count += 3; # $count will contain the value 8

- -= (subtraction-assignment): subtracts a value from an existing variable.

Example:

my $total = 20;

$total -= 5; # $total will contain the value 15

- *= (multiplication-assignment): multiplies a variable by a value.

Example:

my $result = 3;

$result *= 4; # $result will contain the value 12

- /= (division-assignment): divides a variable by a value.

Example:

my $quantity = 10;

$quantity /= 2; # $quantity will contain the value 5

Concatenation operators:

Concatenation operators are used to join two

or more strings into a new string. In Perl, the concatenation operator is the dot (.). Here is an example of how the concatenation operator works in Perl:

Example:

my $str1 = "Hello, ";

my $str2 = "world!";

my $message = $str1 . $str2; # $message will contain "Hello, world!"

These are just some of the most common operators in Perl and their uses. It is important to know how to use operators correctly in Perl to write efficient and readable code. We hope this guide has been helpful for you to better understand how operators work in Perl.

6. Control instructions in Perl (if, else, elsif, switch)

Perl is a powerful scripting language that offers various control structures to manage the flow of the program. The main control instructions in Perl are as follows:

1. if:

The if statement in Perl is used to execute a block of code only if a certain condition is true. The basic syntax of the if statement is as follows:

```perl
if (condition) {
    # code block to execute if the condition is
true
}
```

For example, the following Perl code checks if a number is even or odd:

```perl
my $number = 10;

if ($number % 2 == 0) {
    print "The number $number is even
";
} else {
    print "The number $number is odd
";
}
```

2. else:

The else statement is used in combination with the if statement to execute a block of code if the condition in the if statement is false. The basic syntax of the else statement is as follows:

```perl
if (condition) {

    # code block to execute if the condition is
true

} else {

    # code block to execute if the condition is
false

}
```

For example, the following Perl code checks if a number is positive or negative:

```perl
```

```perl
my $number = -5;

if ($number > 0) {
    print "The number $number is positive
";
} else {
    print "The number $number is negative
";
}
```

3. elsif:

The elsif statement in Perl is used to add additional conditions to the if statement. It can be used successively to handle multiple conditions. The basic syntax of the elsif statement is as follows:

```perl
```

```
if (condition1) {

    # code block to execute if condition1 is true

} elsif (condition2) {

    # code block to execute if condition2 is true

} else {

    # code block to execute if none of the
previous conditions are true

}
```

For example, the following Perl code determines if a number is positive, negative, or zero:

```perl
my $number = 0;

if ($number > 0) {
```

```perl
    print "The number $number is positive
";
} elsif ($number < 0) {

    print "The number $number is negative
";
} else {

    print "The number is zero
";
}
```

4. switch:

Perl does not offer a switch statement like in other programming languages, but you can simulate switch behavior using a series of elsif statements. The basic syntax of a "switch" in Perl would be as follows:

```perl
my $value = 2;
```

```perl
if ($value == 1) {

    # code block for case 1

} elsif ($value == 2) {

    # code block for case 2

} elsif ($value == 3) {

    # code block for case 3

} else {

    # code block for other cases

}
```

For example, the following Perl code simulates a switch to determine the day of the week:

```perl
my $day = "Monday";
```

```perl
if ($day eq "Monday") {

    print "It's Monday
";
} elsif ($day eq "Tuesday") {

    print "It's Tuesday
";
} elsif ($day eq "Wednesday") {

    print "It's Wednesday
";
} elsif ($day eq "Thursday") {

    print "It's Thursday
";
} elsif ($day eq "Friday") {

    print "It's Friday
";
} elsif ($day eq "Saturday") {
```

```perl
    print "It's Saturday
";
} elsif ($day eq "Sunday") {
    print "It's Sunday
";
} else {
    print "Invalid day
";
}
```

Control statements in Perl like if, else, elsif, and the simulated switch example offer the necessary flexibility to handle program flow and execute actions based on specific conditions. By using these statements correctly, you can write cleaner and more organized code in Perl.

7. Data Structures in Perl - Arrays in Perl

Perl is a versatile programming language that offers different types of data structures to store and manage information efficiently. One of the most commonly used data structures in Perl is the array, which allows you to store an ordered sequence of values in a variable.

Arrays in Perl are an ordered collection of elements, accessible through a numerical index that indicates the position of the data within the array. Arrays in Perl start from 0, so the first element has an index of 0, the second element has an index of 1, and so on.

To declare an array in Perl, the symbol @ is used followed by a list of values separated by commas enclosed in square brackets []. For example:

```perl
```

```
my @numbers = (10, 20, 30, 40, 50);
```

In this case, we have created an array named @numbers with five elements containing the values 10, 20, 30, 40, and 50.

To access elements of an array, the access operator [] is used, followed by the index of the desired element. For example:

```perl
my $first_element = $numbers[0]; #
$first_element will be equal to 10
```

In this case, $numbers[0] will return the first element of the array @numbers, which is the value 10.

It is important to note that arrays in Perl can contain elements of different types, such as numbers, strings, other arrays, or even references to functions. For example:

```perl
my @mixed = (10, "hello", 3.14, [1, 2, 3], sub { return "Hello World"; });
```

In this case, we have created an array named @mixed that contains an integer, a string, a decimal number, an array, and an anonymous function.

To add an element to an existing array, the push() function is used, which adds an element to the end of the array. For example:

```perl
```

push(@numbers, 60); # Adds the value 60 to the end of the array @numbers

```
```

To remove an element from the array, the pop() function is used, which removes the last element from the array and returns the deleted value. For example:

```perl
my $last_element = pop(@numbers); # Removes the value 60 from the array @numbers
```
```

Elements can also be added or removed from other positions in the array using the splice() and shift() functions. The splice() function allows adding or removing a specific number of elements from the array starting from a specific position. For example:
```

```perl
splice(@numbers, 2, 0, 35); # Adds the value
35 to position 2 of the array @numbers
```

The shift() function removes the first element
from the array and shifts all other elements
back by one position. For example:

```perl
my $removed_first_element =
shift(@numbers); # Removes the value 10
from the beginning of the array @numbers
```

Lastly, iterating over the elements of an array
is possible using a foreach loop. For example:

```perl
foreach my $num (@numbers) {
    print "$num
";
}
```

This loop iterates over all the elements in the @numbers array and prints them on the screen one per line.

Arrays are essential data structures in Perl that allow storing and managing an ordered set of values efficiently. They are flexible and allow storing elements of different types within the same variable. With array manipulation functions, it is easy and fast to add, remove, or modify elements, making arrays a fundamental tool for developing programs in Perl.

8.Hash in Perl

Hash in Perl is a data structure that allows you to store and manipulate sets of key-value pairs. Keys are unique identifiers used to access the values associated with them. Hashes in Perl are implemented using a data type called "hash reference," which is a reference to a hash table.

To create a hash in Perl, you can use the following code:

```perl
my %hash = (
    key1 => 'value1',
    key2 => 'value2',
    key3 => 'value3'
);
```

In this example, we are creating a hash with three key-value pairs. Key 'key1' has the value 'value1', key 'key2' has the value 'value2', and key 'key3' has the value 'value3'.

To access values within a hash, you can use the hash name followed by the key inside square brackets:

```perl
print $hash{'key1'};  # Prints 'value1'
```

You can also use the "keys" function to get an array containing all the keys of a hash and the "values" function to get an array containing all the values:

```perl
```

```
my @keys = keys %hash;

my @values = values %hash;
```

You can iterate over a hash using a "foreach" loop:

```perl
foreach my $key (keys %hash) {
    print "$key: $hash{$key}\n";
}
```

You can add and modify elements within a hash simply by assigning a value to a specific key:

```perl
```

```perl
$hash{'key4'} = 'value4';

$hash{'key1'} = 'new_value1';
```

You can remove elements from a hash using the "delete" command:

```perl
delete $hash{'key2'};
```

One of the most powerful features of hashes in Perl is the ability to nest complex data structures. You can use a hash reference within another hash to create complex and hierarchical data structures:

```perl
my %nested_hash = (
```

```
   key1 => {

      nested_key1 => 'nested_value1',

      nested_key2 => 'nested_value2'

   },

   key2 => {

      nested_key3 => 'nested_value3',

      nested_key4 => 'nested_value4'

   }

);


print $nested_hash{'key1'}{'nested_key1'};  #
Prints 'nested_value1'

```
```

Hashes in Perl are extremely flexible and
versatile and can be used for a wide range of
applications. They can store structured data,
create fast and efficient lookup tables, and
represent complex objects. Hashes in Perl are
```

a fundamental feature of Perl programming and play a crucial role in data manipulation and processing.

Here is a complete example of how to use a hash in Perl:

```perl
# Creating a hash
my %student = (
    name => 'John Doe',
    age => 20,
    grade => 'A'
);
```

```perl
# Accessing hash values
print "Name: $student{'name'}\n";
print "Age: $student{'age'}\n";
print "Grade: $student{'grade'}\n";


# Modifying a value in the hash
$student{'age'} = 21;


# Adding a new value to the hash
$student{'school'} = 'University';


# Deleting a value from the hash
delete $student{'grade'};


# Iterating through all elements of the hash
foreach my $key (keys %student) {
    print "$key: $student{$key}\n";
```

```perl
}


# Creating a nested hash
my %course = (
    name => 'Programming',
    instructor => 'Jane Smith',
    students => {
        student1 => {
            name => 'Alice',
            age => 22
        },
        student2 => {
            name => 'Bob',
            age => 23
        }
    }
);
```

```
# Accessing values of the nested hash

print "Course name: $course{'name'}\n";

print "Instructor: $course{'instructor'}\n";

print "Student 1 name: $course{'students'}
{'student1'}{'name'}\n";

print "Student 2 age: $course{'students'}
{'student2'}{'age'}\n";

```
```

In this example, we have created a hash named %student with information about a student, such as name, age, and grade. We have also modified and added values to the hash, deleted the grade, and iterated through all elements. We then created a nested hash %course with information about a course, including the course name, instructor, and a hash of students. We then accessed the values of the nested hash using the keys references.
```

Hashes in Perl are a powerful and flexible tool that allows you to store and manipulate data efficiently and in a structured way. With their ability to handle so much information in an organized manner, hashes are an essential tool for programming in Perl.

9. Functions in Perl

Perl is a programming language that provides many useful features for creating and passing parameters to functions. In this article, we will delve into how to create and call a function in Perl, passing parameters to a function, and recursive functions.

Creating and calling a function in Perl:

To create a function in Perl, you can use the following syntax:

```perl
sub function_name {
  # function body
}
```

For example, to create a simple function that prints "Hello, World!", you can use the following code:

```perl
sub print_hello {
  print "Hello, World!\n";
}
```

To call the newly created function, you can write the following code:

```perl
print_hello();
```

This code will print "Hello, World!" when executed.

Passing parameters to a function in Perl:

To pass parameters to a function in Perl, you can use the arguments provided within parentheses when calling the function. For example, if we want to create a function that prints a custom message, we can do it like this:

```perl
sub print_message {
  my ($message) = @_;
  print "$message
";
}
```

```perl
print_message("This is a custom message");
```

In this example, the variable $message contains the value passed to the function when called. When passing the parameter to the function, make sure to enclose it in parentheses and separate it from other parameters with a comma.

Recursive functions in Perl with examples:

Recursive functions are functions that call themselves. They can be useful for solving problems that can be divided into smaller subproblems. Here is an example of a recursive function in Perl that calculates the factorial of a number:

```perl
sub factorial {
```

```perl
my $number = shift;

if ($number == 0) {

  return 1;

} else {

  return $number * factorial($number - 1);

}

}


print factorial(5);  # output: 120
```

In this example, the factorial function calls itself until the number passed as a parameter reaches the value 0. When $number is equal to 0, the function returns 1. Otherwise, the function recursively calculates the factorial by multiplying the current number by the factorial of the previous number.

Recursive functions can be more complex and require more attention to avoid infinite loops.

It is important to ensure clear termination conditions to avoid this issue.

In conclusion, functions in Perl allow for efficient organization and reusability of code. Whether they are simple or complex functions, they can be created, called, and used effectively to solve a variety of problems. Parameter passing and recursive functions are some of the features that make Perl a powerful and flexible language for software development.

10. File Manipulation in Perl

File manipulation in Perl is one of the most common and utilized functions within programs written in this language. To manipulate a file correctly within a Perl program, it is necessary to know the various operations that can be performed on files, such as opening and closing, reading and writing, and advanced operations.

Firstly, it is important to learn how to open and close a file in Perl. To open a file in Perl, the "open" function is used. This function requires two parameters: the first one is the name of the file to open, and the second is the mode in which to open the file. The mode can be read ("r"), write ("w"), or append ("a"). For example, to open a file in write mode, the following code is used:

```
```

```
open(my $file, '>', 'file.txt') or die "Unable to
open file: $!";
```
```

In this example, the open function opens the "file.txt" file in write mode and returns a file handle that is stored in the variable $file. If the file cannot be opened correctly, an error message is generated with die.

Once the file has been successfully opened, it is possible to write inside the file using the "print" function. For example, to write a string inside the file, the following code is used:

```

```
print $file "This is an example of writing
inside a file in Perl.";
```
```
```

In this example, the print function writes the string inside the file using the file handle stored in the variable $file.

To close a file in Perl, the "close" function is used. This function requires one parameter, which is the file handle to close. For example, to close the previously opened file, the following code is used:

```
close $file;
```

This closing of the file is important to ensure that all changes made to the file are saved correctly and that resources are released.

It is also possible to read the content of a file in Perl using the "open" function. To read a file in Perl, the "open" function is used in read mode. For example, to read the content of a file, the following code is used:

```
open(my $file, '<', 'file.txt') or die "Unable to open file: $!";
while (my $line = <$file>) {
    print $line;
}
close $file;
```

In this example, the open function opens the "file.txt" file in read mode, and a while loop is used to read each line of the file using the "<>" operator. Each line is then printed on the screen using the print function.

Advanced file operations in Perl include handling binary files, temporary files, and advanced manipulation of large files. To handle binary files, the "b" mode can be used with the open function. For example, to open a binary file, the following code is used:

```
open(my $file, 'b', 'file.bin') or die "Unable to open binary file: $!";
```

It is important to note that the "b" mode is only available on Microsoft Windows platforms and is not necessary on other operating systems such as Linux or macOS.

To handle temporary files in Perl, the File::Temp module can be used. This module provides functions for creating temporary files safely and managing them afterward. For example, to create a temporary file, the following code is used:

```
use File::Temp;

my $tempfile = File::Temp->new();

print $tempfile "This is a temporary file.";
```

In this example, the File::Temp module is used to create a temporary file, and the "print" function is used to write inside the temporary file.

Lastly, for manipulation of large files in Perl, the Tie::File module can be used. This module provides a convenient interface for reading and writing large files while keeping only the parts of the file that are currently in use in memory. For example, to use the Tie::File module, the following code is used:

```
use Tie::File;

tie my @file, 'Tie::File', 'file.txt';

foreach my $line (@file) {

    print $line;

}
```

In this example, the Tie::File module is used to read the content of the "file.txt" file while keeping only the parts of the file in memory that are currently needed. The foreach loop is used to iterate over each line of the file and print it on the screen.

File manipulation in Perl can be done easily and efficiently using the various functions and modules available in this language. Knowing the different operations that can be performed on files in Perl is essential for developing efficient programs that require file manipulation.

11. Regular expressions in Perl

A regular expression, also known as regex or regexp, is a sequence of characters that defines a search pattern. It is used to identify certain patterns within a text string. Regular expressions are extremely useful for conducting searches, validity checks, and substitutions on text in an efficient and elegant manner.

Perl is one of the programming languages that has built-in support for regular expressions. Thanks to its powerful syntax and the numerous features provided by regular expressions, Perl is widely used for manipulating and analyzing text in an advanced way.

The simplest way to use a regular expression in Perl is to use the "=~" operator along with a regular pattern enclosed between two slashes "/". For example, the following Perl code checks if the string "hello world" contains the word "hello":

```perl
my $str = "hello world";
if ($str =~ /hello/) {
    print "The string contains the word 'hello'\n";
}
```

Regular expressions in Perl support various metacharacters and substitution commands that allow for creating more complex patterns and performing advanced operations on text.

Some of the most commonly used metacharacters in Perl are:

1. "." - Represents any character.

2. "^" - Indicates the beginning of a string.

3. "$" - Indicates the end of a string.

4. "*" - Represents zero or more occurrences of the preceding character.

5. "+" - Represents one or more occurrences of the preceding character.

6. "?" - Represents zero or one occurrence of the preceding character.

7. "[]" - Represents a set of characters.

8. "{}" - Specifies the exact number of occurrences of a character.

9. "|" - Represents logical OR between two patterns.

10. "\d" - Represents any numeric character.

11. "\w" - Represents any alphanumeric character.

For example, the following Perl code uses some of these metacharacters to search for a

3-character alphanumeric sequence within a string:


```perl
my $str = "abc123def";
if ($str =~ /\w{3}/) {
    print "The string contains a 3-character alphanumeric sequence
";
}
```

Substitution commands allow for modifying a text string based on a regular pattern. In Perl, the substitution command is executed using the "s///" operator, followed by the search pattern, the replacement pattern, and any options.

For example, the following Perl code replaces the word "dog" with the word "cat" within a string:

```perl
my $str = "My dog is very friendly";
$str =~ s/dog/cat/;
print $str;
```

Another very useful feature of regular expressions in Perl is the ability to capture specific portions of text using parentheses "()". These captures can be used later in the code to perform more complex operations.

For example, the following Perl code captures an integer within a string and prints it on the screen:

```perl
my $str = "The price is 100 euros";
if ($str =~ /(\d+)/) {
    my $price = $1;
    print "The price is $price euros
";
}
```

Regular expressions in Perl are an extremely powerful tool for manipulating text in an advanced way. Thanks to the numerous metacharacters and substitution commands available, it is possible to create complex patterns and perform sophisticated operations on text strings in an elegant and efficient manner.

12.Modules and CPAN in Perl

CPAN, which stands for Comprehensive Perl Archive Network, is a large online archive that contains thousands of modules, scripts, and documentation for the Perl programming language. It is an essential tool for Perl developers as it allows them to easily integrate functionalities from modules developed by other programmers into their projects, saving time and effort in developing new solutions.

Installing CPAN modules in Perl is a fairly simple process and can be done in several ways. The most common method is to use the CPAN command from the command line. To do this, simply type "cpan" in the shell and follow the instructions to install the desired module. The CPAN command will automatically search for and download the required module from the network and install it on the system.

Another method to install CPAN modules is to use the Perl module installation tool called "cpanm". This tool is faster and easier to use compared to CPAN and allows for more efficient installation of modules. To use cpanm, just type "cpanm module_name" in the shell and the module will be automatically downloaded and installed on the system.

Once the CPAN module is installed, you can use it in your Perl scripts by including it with the "use" directive at the beginning of the code. For example, if you want to use the Math::BigFloat module in your script, simply include the following line of code:

```perl
use Math::BigFloat;
```

This way, the Math::BigFloat module will be loaded and available for use within the script.

It is important to note that you can use multiple modules in the same script by including multiple "use" directives at the beginning of the program.

In addition to using modules available on CPAN, you can also create your own custom Perl modules to extend the language's functionalities. Creating a Perl module is quite simple and only requires a few lines of code. Here is an example of how to create a custom Perl module called "MyModule.pm":

```perl
package MyModule;


use strict;
use warnings;


sub hello {
```

```perl
    my $name = shift;

    print "Hello, $name!\n";

}


1;
```

In this example, we have created a module called MyModule that contains a function called hello which takes a name parameter and prints a greeting message. To use this module within another Perl script, simply include the following line of code:

```perl
use MyModule;


MyModule::hello("Alice");
```

This line of code will print "Hello, Alice!" on the screen using the hello function defined in the MyModule module.

In conclusion, CPAN modules are a valuable tool for Perl developers that allow for easy integration of functionalities developed by other programmers into their projects. Installing CPAN modules is simple and can be done using the cpan or cpanm commands from the command line. Furthermore, you can create your own custom Perl modules to extend the language's functionalities. These modules can be used in Perl scripts by including them with the "use" directive at the beginning of the code.

13. Security in Perl - best practices to ensure Perl code security - common vulnerabilities to avoid in Perl

Perl is a versatile and powerful programming language that is used for a variety of purposes, including web application development and data management. However, like any other programming language, Perl also has vulnerabilities that can compromise the security of the code. In this article, we will explore best practices to ensure Perl code security and common vulnerabilities to avoid.

Best practices to ensure Perl code security:

1. Use strict and warnings: One of the first things to do when writing Perl code is to enable the strict and warnings directives. This helps identify potential errors in the code and ensure greater consistency in its functionality.

Example:

```perl
use strict;
use warnings;
```

2. Input validation: It is essential to validate all input received from the client to prevent injection attacks. For example, if accepting input from a web form, it is important to validate the data before processing it.

Example:

```perl
my $username = $cgi->param('username');
if ($username =~ /^[a-zA-Z0-9_]+$/) {
  # Process the input
```

```
} else {

  # Handle invalid input

}
```
```

3. Limit privileges: When writing code that requires access to sensitive resources, it is advisable to limit the application's privileges to ensure that only what is strictly necessary is executed.

4. Output sanitization: Before returning data to the user, it is important to sanitize the output to prevent Cross-Site Scripting (XSS) attacks. This can be done using escape functions like `HTML::Entities` or `CGI::Escape`.

Example:
```

```perl
use CGI::Escape qw();
print CGI::Escape::escapeHTML($output);
```

5. Use security modules: Perl offers a wide range of modules that help ensure code security. Some examples include `CGI`, `CGI::Session`, and `CGI::Ajax`.

Common vulnerabilities to avoid in Perl:

1. Malicious code injection: One of the most common vulnerabilities in Perl is the injection of malicious code into variables. This can allow an attacker to execute harmful code on the server.

Example:

```perl
my $input = $cgi->param('input');
eval $input;
```

2. File manipulation: File manipulation is another common vulnerability in Perl. When working with files, it is important to validate and sanitize file names to prevent directory traversal attacks.

Example:

```perl
my $filename = $cgi->param('filename');
if ($filename =~ /^[\w\.-]+$/) {
  open my $fh, '>', $filename or die "Unable to open file: $!";
}
```

```
```

3. Password management: Password management is another critical area where security errors can easily occur. It is important to securely store and encrypt passwords to prevent brute force or dictionary attacks.

Example:

```perl
use Digest::MD5 qw(md5_hex);

my $password_hash = md5_hex($password);
```

4. SQL Injection: User-provided input can be used to execute SQL Injection attacks. It is important to use parameterized queries or modules like `DBI` to prevent this type of attack.

Example:

```perl
my $id = $cgi->param('id');

my $sth = $dbh->prepare("SELECT * FROM users WHERE id = ?");

$sth->execute($id);
```

Ensuring Perl code security requires adopting best practices and awareness of common vulnerabilities. By using validation techniques, output sanitization, and privilege limitation, it is possible to write secure and reliable Perl code. By avoiding vulnerabilities such as malicious code injection, file manipulation, and SQL Injection, the risk of compromising the security of your system can be reduced.

14.Debugging and testing in Perl - debugging tools available in Perl - techniques for script testing

Debugging and testing are two crucial phases in software development, helping to identify and correct errors and defects in the code. In this article, we will discuss how to implement debugging and testing in Perl, a widely used scripting language for file management and web application development.

Let's start with debugging, which is the process of identifying and resolving errors in the code. Perl provides several tools for debugging, which help to simplify and speed up this process. One of the main debugging tools in Perl is the `Carp` module, which allows for detailed reporting of errors and warnings, indicating the location of the problem in the code. By using the `carp()` and `croak()` functions, it is possible to customize debug information for better error understanding.

Another important tool for debugging in Perl is the `Data::Dumper` module, which allows for clear visualization of data structure and variables used in the code. By using the `Dumper()` function, it is possible to print the content of a complex variable, such as an array or hash, on the screen to verify the correct functioning of the code.

For interactive debugging, one can use Perl's built-in debugger, called `Perl Debug`. This tool allows for step-by-step code execution, inserting breakpoints at specific points to analyze the program flow and identify any errors. By using control commands such as `n` to move to the next step and `c` to continue execution, it is possible to inspect variables, modify code in real-time, and solve problems.

In addition to debugging tools, it is important to test the code to ensure that it works correctly in different scenarios and conditions. Perl offers various techniques for testing, including the `Test::More` module, which allows for creating automated tests to verify the behavior of functions and modules written in Perl. By using the `ok()`, `is()`, and `like()` functions, it is possible to define expectations and check that the code returns the expected results.

Below, we provide an example of how to use the `Test::More` module to test a simple function written in Perl:

```perl
use strict;

use warnings;

use Test::More;
```

```perl
sub sum {

  my ($a, $b) = @_;

  return $a + $b;

}


plan tests => 3;


ok(sum(2, 3) == 5, 'The sum of 2 and 3 is 5');

ok(sum(0, 0) == 0, 'The sum of 0 and 0 is 0');

ok(sum(-1, -1) == -2, 'The sum of -1 and -1 is -2');


done_testing();
```

In this example, we define a `sum` function
that returns the sum of two numbers. We use
the `Test::More` module to verify that the
function produces the expected results in three

different cases. With the command `plan tests => 3`, we indicate that we are running three tests, and with the `ok()` functions, we check that the sum of the numbers passed to the function corresponds to the expected result.

In addition to the `Test::More` module, other testing tools and frameworks can be used in Perl, such as `Test::Simple`, `Test::Class`, and `Test::Unit`, which offer advanced functionalities for unit testing, mock testing, and interface testing.

In conclusion, debugging and testing are essential to ensure the quality and correctness of code written in Perl. By using available debugging tools and following appropriate testing techniques, it is possible to identify and correct errors effectively, ensuring robust and reliable code.

15. Examples of applications made with Perl

In this detailed guide, we will explore how to create an application with Perl. Perl is a high-level programming language that is widely used for web application development, system scripting, and process automation. It is known for its flexibility and power, and is a popular choice among programmers for its ability to handle a wide range of tasks.

To get started, make sure you have Perl installed on your system. You can download and install Perl from the official website or use a package manager if you are on a Unix-like system. Once Perl is installed, you can start writing code for your application.

Below, I show a simple example of code for an application written in Perl:

```
`` `

#!/usr/bin/perl

use strict;
use warnings;

# Define a simple function to greet the user
sub greet {
    my $name = shift;
    print "Hello, $name!\n";
}

# Ask the user for their name
print "What is your name? ";
my $user_name = <STDIN>;
chomp $user_name;
```

```perl
# Call the greet function passing the user's name
greet($user_name);
```

In this example, we are defining a function called "greet" that takes an argument (the user's name) and prints it to the screen with a greeting message. We then ask the user to input their name using the <STDIN> function and chomp the newline. Finally, we call the "greet" function passing the user's name inputted by the user.

This is a very simple example of an application written in Perl. However, Perl can be used to create much more complex and powerful applications. For example, you can develop web applications using Perl with frameworks like Mojolicious or Catalyst.

To implement a more sophisticated

application, you can use CPAN (Comprehensive Perl Archive Network) modules that offer a wide library of third-party modules to extend Perl's functionalities. You can install CPAN modules using the command cpan install ModuleName from the command line.

Additionally, you can use Perl to interact with databases, read and write files, perform network operations, and much more. The power of Perl lies in its ability to efficiently and concisely handle a wide range of tasks.

Here is an example of code showing how to connect to a MySQL database using Perl:

```
```

#!/usr/bin/perl

use strict;
```
```

```perl
use warnings;

use DBI;


# Parameters for connecting to the database

my $database = 'database_name';

my $host = 'localhost';

my $port = '3306';

my $username = 'username';

my $password = 'password';


# Connect to the database

my $dbh = DBI-
>connect("DBI:mysql:database=$database;ho
st=$host;port=$port", $username, $password)
or die "Unable to connect to the database:
$DBI::errstr";


# Prepare an SQL query

my $query = "SELECT * FROM table";
```

```perl
# Execute the query

my $sth = $dbh->prepare($query);

$sth->execute();


# Get the query result

while(my $row = $sth->fetchrow_arrayref) {

    print join("\t", @$row)."\n";

}


# Close the database connection

$sth->finish();

$dbh->disconnect();

```

In this code, we are using the DBI (Database Interface) module to connect to a MySQL database and execute an SQL query to retrieve data from a table. It is important to properly manage the database connection and resources to avoid memory leaks and potential security issues.

Perl is a powerful and versatile language that can be used for a wide range of applications. Knowing Perl can be very useful for developers working on projects that require process automation, system scripting, web application development, and much more.

To illustrate how one could create an application with Perl, we can imagine wanting to create a simple program that reads a text file, counts how many times a specific word appears within the text, and returns the positions where the word is found.

Here is an example of Perl code that implements this functionality:

```perl
#!/usr/bin/perl

use strict;
use warnings;

# Open the text file for reading
open(my $file, "<", "text.txt") or die "Unable to open file: $!";

# Read the content of the file
my $text = do { local $/; <$file> };

# Close the file
close($file);
```

```perl
# Define the word for which we want to count
occurrences

my $word = "Lorem";


# Initialize a hash to store the positions where
the word appears

my %positions;


# Use a regex to find all occurrences of the
word in the text
while ($text =~ /\b$word\b/g) {

    my $position = pos($text) - length($word)
+ 1;

    push @{$positions{$word}}, $position;

}


# Print the positions where the word appears
foreach my $position
```

```perl
(@{$positions{$word}}) {

    print "The word '$word' appears at position $position

";

}
```

In this example, the code opens a text file named "text.txt", reads its content, and stores the text in a variable. Then, the word "Lorem" that we want to count occurrences of is defined.

Using a regex, the code searches for all occurrences of the word in the text and stores the positions where it is found in the %positions hash.

Finally, the code prints the positions where the word appears in the text.

This is just a small example of what can be done with Perl. The language offers many advanced features for manipulating data, managing files, communicating with databases, and much more.

Perl is especially appreciated for its ease in handling regular expressions and creating powerful and compact scripts for automating repetitive tasks.

Whether you are developing a simple utility or a complex web application, Perl is an excellent choice for a wide range of projects. Its extensive ecosystem of modules and libraries makes it possible to create practically any type of application with ease and precision.

Additionally, Perl has an active community and numerous forums where developers can share knowledge, solve problems, and collaborate to improve the language and its libraries.

In this code, we are using the DBI (Database Interface) module to connect to a MySQL database and execute an SQL query to retrieve data from a table. It is important to properly manage the database connection and resources to avoid memory leaks and potential security issues.

Perl is a powerful and versatile language that can be used for a wide range of applications. Knowing Perl can be very useful for developers working on projects that require process automation, system scripting, web application development, and much more.

To illustrate how one could create an application with Perl, we can imagine wanting to create a simple program that reads a text file, counts how many times a specific word appears within the text, and returns the positions where the word is found.

Here is an example of Perl code that

implements this functionality:

```perl
#!/usr/bin/perl

use strict;
use warnings;

# Open the text file for reading
open(my $file, "<", "text.txt") or die "Unable to open file: $!";

# Read the content of the file
my $text = do { local $/; <$file> };

# Close the file
close($file);
```

```perl
# Define the word for which we want to count
occurrences

my $word = "Lorem";


# Initialize a hash to store the positions where
the word appears

my %positions;


# Use a regex to find all occurrences of the
word in the text

while ($text =~ /\b$word\b/g) {

    my $position = pos($text) - length($word)
+ 1;

    push @{$positions{$word}}, $position;

}


# Print the positions where the word appears

foreach my $position
```

```perl
(@{$positions{$word}}) {

    print "The word '$word' appears at position $position

";

}
```

In this example, the code opens a text file named "text.txt", reads its content, and stores the text in a variable. Then, the word "Lorem" that we want to count occurrences of is defined.

Using a regex, the code searches for all occurrences of the word in the text and stores the positions where it is found in the %positions hash.

Finally, the code prints the positions where the word appears in the text.

This is just a small example of what can be done with Perl. The language offers many advanced features for manipulating data, managing files, communicating with databases, and much more.

Perl is especially appreciated for its ease in handling regular expressions and creating powerful and compact scripts for automating repetitive tasks.

Whether you are developing a simple utility or a complex web application, Perl is an excellent choice for a wide range of projects. Its extensive ecosystem of modules and libraries makes it possible to create practically any type of application with ease and precision.

Additionally, Perl has an active community and numerous forums where developers can share knowledge, solve problems, and collaborate to improve the language and its libraries.

Index

1.Introduction to Perl pg.4

2. Perl Installation Guide pg.8

3.Basic Perl Syntax pg.12

4.Variables and Data Types in Perl pg.19

5.Operators in Perl pg.24

6. Control instructions in Perl (if, else, elsif, switch) pg.36

7. Data Structures in Perl - Arrays in Perl pg.45

8.Hash in Perl pg.51

9. Functions in Perl pg.61

10. File Manipulation in Perl pg.67

11. Regular expressions in Perl pg.75

12.Modules and CPAN in Perl pg.82

13. Security in Perl - best practices to ensure Perl code security - common vulnerabilities to avoid in Perl pg.87

14.Debugging and testing in Perl - debugging tools available in Perl - techniques for script testing pg. 94

15. Examples of applications made with Perl pg.99